Help ???
Help !!!

Solving
Learning Problems
{Even Dyslexia}

by
David Conway

Illustrated by
Lawrence T. Randall

Nancibell® Inc.

Designed by David Conway and Lawrence T. Randall
Cover Drawing by Phyllis Lindamood

Publisher Cataloging in Publication Data

Conway, David
      Help ??? Help !!! Solving Learning Problems
      {Even Dylexia}

1, Learning. 2, Dyslexia. 3, Education. I Title

Library of Congress Catalog Card Number: 91-66597

ISBN: 0-9630681-6-4

Help ???

Help !!!

Solving
Learning Problems
{Even Dyslexia}

Dedication

To education's walking wounded.

The students, parents, and teachers who suffer when education does not produce learning.

Acknowlededement

I cannot hope to list all those who helped to make this book a reality. Even so, there are some people I feel I especially need to thank directly. Charles and Patricia Lindamood, Nanci Bell, and Phyllis Lindamood are the talented people who created the programs covered in this book. Kimberly, my wife, deserves special thanks for her kind support. Noble Sprunger's contributions of support and confidence were invaluable. Many thanks must go to the publisher and main editor, without their patient, but relentless, help there would be no book. To all the others I haven't named, please accept my thanks and enjoy the final product. Finally, I want to thank the source of all things, God.

Preface

If you know ten people then you most likely know at least three people who have trouble learning. They may have a problem reading and spelling. It might be hard for them to understand what they hear or read. Maybe they struggle with handwriting and simple drawing. Just one of these basic skills may be hard for them, or they may struggle with all three. Trouble with one, or all, of these basic skills makes learning hard for at least three out of every ten people you know.

illustration #1
Some people enjoy learning, some just wish it would go away.

Basic skills are important in modern life. Modern human beings need to read and spell. People also need to understand what they read or hear in modern society. There are radio and television speeches, newspapers, faxes, tax laws, banking directions and hundreds of other things to listen to or read. People need to understand these words and the words coming at them from other places too. Modern societies also use signs and visual symbols, lots of them. People in the society need to use these signs and visual symbols easily and quickly.

For over ten years I have worked with people needing help with one, or all, of the basic skills. Missing one, or all, of these skills usually made their lives hard. School and education were especially hard for them. When we finished, many of these people shared a feeling of relief and anger. Relief because they now had the skill, or skills, they needed. Anger because they could have had the skill sooner if someone had known what to do. These people often said to me, "why don't more people know about this work?" So, I've written this book to tell about the help possible for people with learning problems. Help that works even for people told they have "dyslexia."

The programs I'll talk about help people develop the basic skills of comprehending, reading and spelling, and drawing. I'll tell you about each program and how it works. Also, I'll tell you about some people I've worked with over the years. You may see yourself, or a friend, in the same situation as one of these people.

The programs are known in Australia, Canada, England, Ireland, New Zealand, the Cayman Islands, Bermuda, and the United States. In spite of this wide distribution, readers who are scholars will find few statistics, studies, or other trappings of an educational text. This book is for people who need help with learning, or who know someone that needs help. Piles of numbers and formal research jargon makes it harder for these people to find help. If you are interested in research or statistics, you can ask for that kind of information in the Appendix by contacting the author.

illustration #2
Trying to find help in research books

If you have trouble learning, read Section 1, or have a friend read it and tell you about it. If you know somebody who has trouble learning, tell them about this book and read on to see for yourself the difference that can be made in their* life. There is no reason for most people to struggle with learning basic skills. You, or the people you know, may not have to spend a lifetime working around a learning problem. Things might change for you, just like they changed for the people you'll meet as you read.

*Through a strict interpretation of grammar some readers will find this use of "their," and later uses of "they," incorrect. I'm using these words because of gender issues. Terms like he/she, s/he, or sometimes she and other times he, are frustrating to many readers and to me. Since both sexes have learning problems, the language in this book tries to be gender neutral. There is precedence in other writings for a none plural use of "their" and "they." So I hope you find the more gender neutral language adds to your enjoyment. DC

CONTENTS

Preface   7

Section 1   LEARNING   13

   Chapter 1 Comprehension   21
             How we do it and how to learn to do it

   Chapter 2 Phonics   41
             Sound and Dyslexia

   Chapter 3 Drawing and Handwriting   61
             So easy and yet so hard

   Chapter 4 Learning   77
             What can happen when people can learn

   Chapter 5 Questions and Answers   91
             What people often ask

Section 2   EDUCATION   103

   Chapter 6 The Educational World   109
             Education is really two worlds

   Chapter 7 Numbers   117
             Doing it by the numbers, for the numbers

   Chapter 8 A Real Solution   131
             Learning and Education can add up

APPENDIX   143

Index   147

Illustrations

illustration #01 -- Page #07 • illustration #26 -- Page #62
illustration #02 -- Page #09 • illustration #27 -- Page #63
illustration #03 -- Page #15 • illustration #28 -- Page #69
illustration #04 -- Page #16 • illustration #29 -- Page #70
illustration #05 -- Page #18 • illustration #30 -- Page #72
illustration #06 -- Page #20 • illustration #31 -- Page #73
illustration #07 -- Page #25 • illustration #32 -- Page #74
illustration #08 -- Page #26 • illustration #33 -- Page #75
illustration #09 -- Page #31 • illustration #34 -- Page #77
illustration #10 -- Page #34 • illustration #35 -- Page #78
illustration #11 -- Page #35 • illustration #36 -- Page #81
illustration #12 -- Page #36 • illustration #37 -- Page #83
illustration #13 -- Page #37 • illustration #38 -- Page #84
illustration #14 -- Page #37 • illustration #39 -- Page #89
illustration #15 -- Page #38 • illustration #40 -- Page 110
illustration #16 -- Page #38 • illustration #41 -- Page 111
illustration #17 -- Page #43 • illustration #42 -- Page 112
illustration #18 -- Page #50 • illustration #43 -- Page 114
illustration #19 -- Page #50 • illustration #44 -- Page 115
illustration #20 -- Page #51 • illustration #45 -- Page 118
illustration #21 -- Page #54 • illustration #46 -- Page 121
illustration #22 -- Page #55 • illustration #47 -- Page 122
illustration #23 -- Page #56 • illustration #48 -- Page 129
illustration #24 -- Page #57 • illustration #49 -- Page 132
illustration #25 -- Page #58 • illustration #50 -- Page 134

Section One
Learning

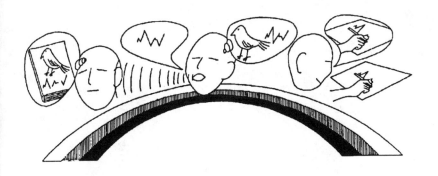

Learning is the most important thing people do. From birth to death humans are doing some kind of learning. To help this important activity most societies have education systems. The education system teaches people a few basic skills. Then the people use the basic skills to learn other information. Much effort goes into teaching the basic skills since most future education depends on them.

illustration # 3
Education starts with learning basic skills.

In spite of education's efforts, and other efforts, millions of people struggle, unsuccessfully, to learn basic reading and spelling, comprehension, and visual-motor skills like handwriting. So many people have trouble that communities around the world are trying to do something about it. In the United States, for example, there is some kind of extra learning help for people, besides what is in the schools, in almost every town.

illustration #4
For some, education stays at learning the basics.

But many who try to get extra help learning the basic skills end up frustrated. They find that the methods used to help them are ones that have already failed them. Also, these people often hear messages they have heard before. They have heard school officials and parents say: "if you'll just concentrate more, pay closer attention, you can learn," or "if you'll just try harder, you can get it," or "you're doing a good job, but you're not working up to your potential," or "if you'll take this medicine you'll be able to pay attention better and that will help you learn." The places offering extra learning help also, often, offer the same old messages: "if you'll really try you'll notice a difference," or "if you'll just concentrate more you can learn to do this," or "if you'll motivate yourself you can do these things," or "you're an adult now, if you'll just work at it you'll get it."

Even after getting extra help many of the people who improve are still frustrated. All the extra work did not make them independent. They still need another person to check their work. They still must depend on someone else to help them spell a word, or help them be sure they understand what they read and hear.

People who have trouble learning, after working at education, don't need more of the same old activities. They don't need more phonics or spelling drills, more work with sight words, or more language practice. They don't need to answer more questions about what they read or hear, or do more math drills. People in school have done such drills for years. Some have done these things through years of college and/or hours of extra tutoring. If the same old activities were going to make a real difference, they would have already solved the person's learning problem.

The methods described in this section are different. They are not the same old activities. They are different and, to date, reliable approaches to helping end reading and spelling troubles {dyslexia}, comprehension troubles. and visual-motor troubles. These methods deal with why people who have learning problems are not successful in reading and spelling, comprehending, or doing handwriting and drawing.

People teaching the basic skills usually assume an individual trying to learn has all the abilities needed to learn successfully. The methods in this book deal with basic abilities, needed for successful learning, that are overlooked by most education systems. The methods help develop "precursor" abilities. Abilities a person needs first, for independent and successful learning.

Individuals who have not fully developed some, or all, of these

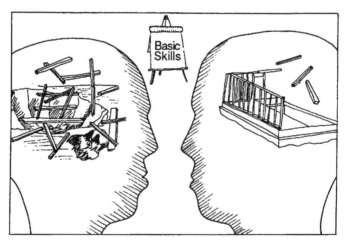

illustration #5
Basic skills need some even more basic abilities as a foundation

"precursor" abilities are often incorrectly labelled as having another problem. Sadly, they may be told they are bad, or stupid, or unwilling to learn. Even when a person with learning problems is loved and not told anything negative, they still know something is wrong. The most loving and kind family or school will not change the fact that if you cannot read, then you cannot read street signs, job applications, or direction manuals. In fact, you cannot read any of the things you need to read to get around in the world. All the love and kindly support in the world cannot help persons unable to read or understand language live their lives in mature, independent ways. In a world where the basic skills are more frequently needed, people who have learning problems, even loved and supported ones, know they are in trouble.

To date, everyone going through the methods in this book, done correctly, has been able to develop the "precursor" abilities. Most have then used their new abilities to improve on, and even become independent with, reading and spelling, comprehending, and handwriting or drawing. This consistent success is why the methods, as described in this book, are not more of the same old thing. Instead, they are breakthroughs in the understanding of the basic abilities people need to learn effectively. If all students could have these methods in their first years of school, the impact would be unbelievable. The methods covered in this first section offer the chance for a revolution in the world of education.

illustration #6
What education can be, when students have the abilities they need for successful learning.

Chapter One

Comprehension

How we do it and how to learn to do it

The first duty of education is to develop comprehension. Education systems help students learn. The most basic skill a student needs, to succeed in learning, is the ability to understand and interpret {comprehend} language and numbers.

JENNY

Jenny is seventeen years old and in the twelfth grade in the United States. She is very quiet and often has a set expression to her face.

Jenny is pretty, with dark eyes, dark hair and, though she doesn't have much "sparkle," a very attractive general appearance.

Early in her twelfth grade year Jenny took some tests. One test measured word attack, how well Jenny figured out words she had never seen before. Her word attack was at a twelfth grade level. Another test measured her ability to recognize words on a list. Jenny could recognize words at an end of eleventh grade level. She also spelled at an end of eleventh grade level.

Besides reading and spelling the tests checked other areas of learning. For instance, Jenny's vocabulary was at a seventeen year old level. She scored at a twelfth grade level in paragraph reading. She read the paragraphs fluently and with expression. In other words, she had emphasis in her voice tones and used the punctuation just as it was meant to be used.

The tests showed that Jenny read and spelled words like she should for a person at the start of twelfth grade. She could even figure out words she had never seen before. In short, Jenny had the basic reading and spelling skills she needed to learn. With these good basic skills Jenny probably seems like a person who would do well in education.

But Jenny took all the tests listed above because she was not going to graduate from high school. Though she seemed to have the basic skills most people think are needed for success in education, Jenny had failed many of her past classes. Now, in her last year of high school, she was failing every class.

Some questions might uncover why Jenny was failing. First, how did Jenny think she was doing in school. {Maybe she thought she was doing fine and that was the problem.} When asked she says, "Terrible . . . I always get F's on everything." Well, maybe the problem was study habits; did Jenny study for tests? "Not anymore," she says, " . . . I used to, but it didn't do any good, I still failed the tests." Perhaps the problem was how she studied. Did she only read chapters one time? Jenny says, "I used to read them four or five times, but I still couldn't remember what I read." What about her parents? Maybe she just needed a little help from them but didn't get it. Jenny's father was very frustrated. He said, "I tried and tried to help Jenny. It just never made sense that she could read something easily and not be able to answer even a simple question about it. It was easier to think Jenny just wasn't trying than to believe there was anything wrong with her."

What was the problem? Jenny had good basic reading and spelling skills, but she was not learning. Some of the other tests answered the question. On the paragraph reading test, where Jenny scored at the twelfth grade level in how fast and accurately she read the words, she could not answer recall questions past the third grade level paragraph. On another test of paragraph reading, her comprehension was at the ninth percentile for a person her age. This means she was in the very disabled range. On a third comprehension test she was at the tenth percentile for someone her age.

Just so you know, normal would be between the fortieth to sixtieth percentile and low normal would be between the twentieth to fortieth percentile. Scores at the ninth and tenth percentile mean Jenny had a severe disability even though she read at her grade level.

Jenny's trouble comprehending language showed up in the fourth grade. Her teacher noticed she read very well, but she could not answer questions about what she read. With this teacher's help Jenny spent a lot of time reading and answering questions. Many people, her parents, other teachers, and extra tutors helped her to read and answer questions. But, even with this extra practice, by twelfth grade she still could not comprehend enough of what she read to answer questions correctly.

After the cause of Jenny's problem was recognized, she began the program covered in this chapter. Instead of reading and answering questions like she had done for the last eight years, which had not helped her, Jenny did the steps of the NanciBell® program. In less than four months, when she had to quit because her family moved, she went from comprehension performance at the ninth and tenth percentile to comprehension performance at the thirty-eighth and fortieth percentile.

To do well in life people need to comprehend and interpret the words and numbers used around them. In school students learn more and more words and their meanings. This vocabulary gives them words they can use to describe the world around them. Student's also learn about numbers. They learn to tell if they are looking at house numbers, numbers describing a distance, or numbers for some other purpose. When a person finishes with education society expects them to comprehend language and numbers. Banks, stores, and tax agencies expect people to understand numbers. Military officers expect soldiers to understand orders. Employers expect employees to read signs and understand them. Employees also need to understand oral directions and written memos or instruction manuals.

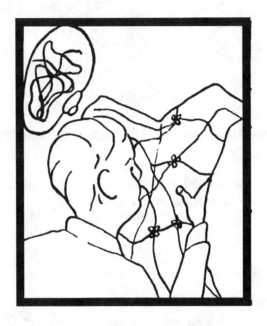

illustration # 7
It can be hard to understand things you read or hear.

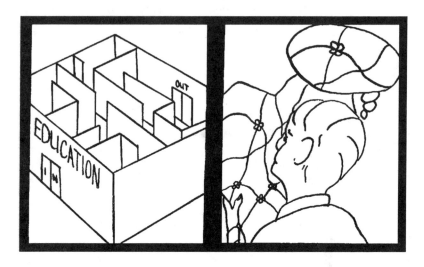

illustration #8
Going through education is supposed to teach you to
understand (comprehend) the words and numbers used
around you.

When a person has the chance to learn language and numbers, but does not comprehend them, their lack of comprehension begins to make problems. The schools and communities can become very frustrated with the person and are, often, uncertain about what to do.

ALBERT

Albert was a seventh grader in a big southwestern city in the United States. His well-to-do parents had him enrolled in one of the best private schools in the area. Albert had such amazing magnetism that, all through his school career, all his classmates and his teachers liked liked him. He was also a very gifted dancer. For example, Albert was the youngest person ever invited to dance in an annual production by the major dance company where he lived.

Besides his natural abilities, Albert was a very disciplined individual. During the school year it was normal for him to spend two hours doing homework, go to a two hour dance workout, and return to home to do another hour or two of school work. Albert spent three and four hours a night on homework because it was hard for him to comprehend language. It took him a long time to understand the things he had to read and to organize the things he had to write.

Albert's parents supported his different interests and, because of his difficulties, got him tutoring help. This meant, in addition to his already busy schedule, Albert squeezed in two or three weekly visits with a tutor. The tutoring services were provided by the most expensive and respected "educational support service" agency in the area. In addition, Albert's father, a former teacher, helped on the days Albert can't get to his tutor.

In spite of four years of this kind of hard work and extra tutoring help, Albert was going to have to leave the private school he was attending. Even with all his effort, Albert's performance on the required homework and class work was so low that he no longer met the school's admission standards.

What was Albert's problem? He read words very easily and spelled well. He just didn't understand or interpret language like it seemed he should. He often didn't follow directions. For example, if he took a test and the directions said to circle the choice that did not match, he might circle all the choices that did match.

Albert was very frustrating to the professionals at his school. Because he got along well with his teachers, and did so well in his classroom social situation, it was impossible to classify him as a problem child. He excelled in dancing and athletics. He put forth such disciplined effort in his school work that everybody saw he wasn't lazy. Albert, for some reason, just didn't get much result from his academic efforts.

KEATS

Keats was a junior in high school and beginning to face problems graduating. She had such a hard time with math and unfamiliar class material that she couldn't keep up with what her school asked her to do. She explains in her own words some of her experience.

"Mrs. Clark, I don't understand this."

"I explained this in class, Keats. You take the mean of the given numbers and divide it by the absolute value of X."

"That's what I don't understand."

"You take the mean of the given numbers and divide it by the absolute value of X. If you would pay closer attention in class, you wouldn't have to come in for extra help."

Keats says, "I used to think I was dumb. For as long as I can remember math teachers have been telling me that I don't work up to my potential in math. They tell me how bright I am and go on about how I shouldn't be having any trouble. They said there was no reason why I shouldn't have been getting A's in the class. 'I know you're a good student because I've heard it from other teachers—so what is going on with you and my class?' The same rule applied for chemistry and other subjects that deal with unfamiliar concepts."

"In the fall of my junior year, I was tested for auditory conceptual function and comprehension skills. Although I got a perfect score on the auditory conceptual function test, I was told that my comprehension skills needed improvement. I was capable of 'seeing' familiar things, which explains why I did well in English and history. Anything like electron loading shells, or functions of X, made no pictures in my mind and were, therefore, undefined and meaningless. I had struggled through math classes by memorizing, memory wasn't enough."

VALARIE

Valarie was the doctor's wife in a small New England town where she lived. She was an accomplished woman. She had a Master's degree in English, three children, and a marriage of thirteen years. Valarie and her husband were beginning to face the possibility of divorce. They couldn't seem to talk anymore. Her husband explained that talking with Valarie was very frustrating. He sometimes had to repeat what he said five or six times, and even then she might not get it. If they went to a movie together she was not able to follow the plot or story line. On television shows, especially if there were flashbacks, Valarie became lost and unable to attend to the show anymore. In the thirteen years of their marriage she had never cracked a joke with her husband. She also never got the point of the jokes he told.

Because they loved each other and wanted to save their marriage, they tried counselling with three different kinds of therapists. Sadly, none of it seemed to make any difference. After a few visits Valarie said that it didn't make sense to go because, most of the time, she couldn't follow what the counselor was talking about.

Each of these people were able and intelligent. But, for some reason, they failed to comprehend language like they needed to for the life they live. All of them had educational opportunities. They even had the advantage of extra educational help when they needed it. Each of them had situations where they could develop and learn. All of them tried to use the chances they had for learning and education.

With all their opportunities and efforts, why was it so difficult for Jenny, Albert, Keats, and Valarie to comprehend? In all the extra help, study skills, their extra effort and self-discipline, what was missing for them, and the many others like them? The ways education usually tries to help comprehension; reading and answering questions, rereading material, taking notes, doing highlighting, asking questions, and talking with teachers, just didn't work for these people. But, when something new came into their situation, just like Jenny, each of the others immediately began to improve in language comprehension. Let's look at the extra something these people, and others like them, need to more fully develop language comprehension.

Words and numbers describe sensory experiences. They describe the world that we see, hear, smell, taste, and feel. Basically the words of language, or the things described by numbers, are connected to something people see or experience. For example, the word "door" means something because people have seen doors, felt doors, or heard the opening and closing of doors. In short, the word "door" has meaning because it connects to things that can be experienced or sensed.

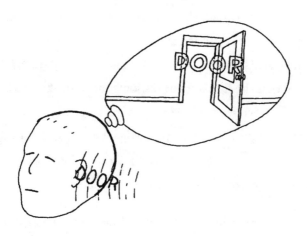

illustration #9
Words work because you "see" in your mind what they mean.

Even less concrete words than "door," like "beauty," get their meaning from sensory experiences. Consciously or unconsciously, every person relates the word "beauty" to some sensory experience. The experience may be a verse of music, a landscape, the look of another person, or the feel of a certain texture. But somewhere, by some chain of connections, even the abstract idea "beauty" ties back to concrete sensory experiences. Even things like quantum physics, and the world it describes with numbers and mathematical operations, finds meaning for its numbers and operations through the sensory reality perceived, or imagined, by a physicist.

The connection of language to sensory experience seems so basic that it is most often not given direct attention in education. But, people like Jenny, Albert, Keats, and Valarie do not easily make the connection of language to sensory experience. Without ties to sensory experience, language represents meaningless junk that a school asks a person to memorize, or that the head office asks someone to do. Unless there are connections between sensory experiences and language, students cannot comprehend and do with their lives what they may wish to do. The basis of comprehension is an ability to connect language to sensory experiences that make it real and understandable.

People like Jenny, Albert, Keats, and Valarie do not easily make the connections by themselves. This means they need to be taught how to connect language to meaningful sensory experiences. Learning to connect language to sensory experience caused Jenny's rapid improvement in comprehension.

People develop the ability to connect language to sensory experiences through the program Visualizing and Verbalizing for Language Comprehension and Thinking by Nanci Bell. Information on the program, and training in it, is available through the Appendix. This program trains individuals to connect to language through visualization. It is the program that made such a difference for Jenny and, as you will see later, also made the difference for Albert, Keats, and Valarie.

This program trains a person to visualize in their mind's eye anything described by language and, then, change their visualization back into language. As simple as this may sound, it is often complex and challenging to learn or teach. For most people the trouble is that they "see" only part of what is being described by the words and never get the whole idea, the "gestalt." Other people must first be trained to see images in their mind's eye. Others can see images, but cannot change their images into words. In spite of different starting points, however, people finish this program able to visualize the meaning of language and verbalize their images.

Briefly, the program follows these steps. A person starts by looking at a picture, something like illustration #10, and describing it to a trained professional, who cannot see the picture. The person describes the picture using words that let the professional see, in their mind's eye, the picture that the person has in front of them. Working through this kind of describing, the professional and the person develop categories that can apply to any picture. Categories like what {is it a table or a dog}, size, shape, and color are identified. Through questions by the professional, the person works toward an ability with words that helps them to "see" the image in their mind's eye. At the same time, they learn to use language to create the image they are seeing in another person's mind.

illustration # 10
A simple drawing with few parts.

When a person can do the above, they are switched from describing given pictures to describing their own images from a single word. The words are carefully picked to connect to something known to the person. This describing, of the image produced by single words, uses the same categories of what, shape, size, etc., developed earlier. Soon, the person's visualizing and verbalizing develop so the professional can "see," from their words, the image the person "sees" in their mind.

Once the person can visualize and easily describe known nouns, they move to short phrases. The phrases are a few words linked in ways that the make the person create and describe a more complex mental image. All the different parts of the image must match the words in the phrase.

A phrase like "a dog ran" makes the person see an image of a dog, like the single word task above. But now the person also needs to visualize the dog in a certain kind of activity.

When a person can easily image a short phrase, the task expands to a sentence, and then to sentence by sentence. At this point the person needs to turn the words into a "concept image" of the gestalt and then verbally describe the concept image in a word summary. Creation of the gestalt image is very important, so the next illustrations help show the process.

illustration # 11
First the person hears, or reads, a
sentence. In this example, the person
listens to a sentence they want to "see."

illustration # 12
Now the person starts to "see" what it means.

First the person thinks about parts of the sentence. For example, the sentence said "loved," that is past tense, so it is probably an older person remembering something from when they were younger. That means, to be sure to get the whole concept, the person making the gestalt image needs to picture an older person moving back to being a younger person.

illustration # 13

The person also needs to "see" the house and the tree
together in order to closely match the sentence.

illustration # 14

The sentence didn't say for sure what kind of swinging
to see, so a decision between possibilities must be
made until more is known.

illustration # 15
Then the images come together to form a gestalt, a concept
image, about what the language in the sentence ment.

illustration # 16
Finally the person turns the concept image back into
language, using their own words.

Once the person can do concept imaging and word summarizing from sentences, they move on to paragraphs, pages, and chapters in books. Finally the person concludes with imaging and summarizing language from class lectures or training talks.

The above is a brief and very simplified description of a unique program. These seemingly simple steps develop the ability to take in language and turn it into something meaningful — comprehension. Concept imagery is a most flexible and powerful way to connect sensory experiences to language. The tremendous power of images linked to language is indirectly recognized every day in such phrases as, "I see what you mean" or "can you see what I'm talking about?"

What can happen when a person completes this program? How can a life change with developing the ability to turn language into concept images and turn concept images back into language? Let's look again at Valarie, Keats, and Albert.

VALARIE

Valarie and her husband, the doctor, are still married. They describe one of the great moments of their relationship as the first time Valarie came home from a clinical session and told her husband a joke. It was the first joke she had ever been able to tell him correctly since it was the first joke she had ever really understood.

Valarie is also enjoying television and movies with her family since she can see the relationships between flashbacks and other parts of the show(s).

KEATS

Keats, the high school junior, says:

"I began to go to one hour visualizing/verbalizing sessions, five days a week. Reading abstract material aloud and forced to describe images was for a long time frustrating and tiring. I usually left with a headache, wanting only to go home and sleep. Initially, I thought the whole thing was a painful waste of time and would never make a difference. It made taking chemistry and algebra even more difficult because I was slowly changing my way of thinking and developing real learning skills. For the first time, I was beginning to actually understand math instead of temporarily memorizing it. As a result, my grades in math and chemistry fell instead of improving. It was not until the summer that I was able to visualize well enough to see everything that I had been missing. At that point, I realized that all the time and frustration that I had put into those ten months was nothing in comparison to what I had been missing my whole life. There had always been something slowing me down. I began to see what possibilities it opened up for me. I am sure that I could not write the quality of fiction that I write now, without having developed these skills. Had I learned to visualize fully before I started high school, the entire four years would have been a worthwhile and more useful experience. Developing visualization skills (i.e., concept imagery) was extraordinarily challenging, but far more rewarding. It is like having the door of your own cage unlocked and opened. It gave me confidence in my own intelligence and a sense of academic achievement."

<u>ALBERT</u>

After Albert completed the visualizing and verbalizing program, he went from C's and D's to the honor roll. He did this at the same school that was going to refuse to admit him because he couldn't keep up with the work requirements. He has continued for the last several years at this school without extra tutorial support. Albert doesn't even get help from his father, the teacher.

Page for

Notes / Comments / Questions

Chapter Two

Phonics
Sounds and Dyslexia

For most people reading and spelling means learning to use letters to show the sounds of their spoken language. Showing sounds with some

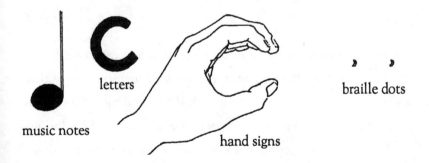

letters

braille dots

music notes

hand signs

illustration # 17
We use many different ways to show sounds.

kind of symbol is so basic that deaf people often learn hand symbols to show sounds they cannot hear. Blind people learn tactile symbols to show sounds, instead of the visual letters generally used in their society.

After persons learn to match a letter, or symbol, to the individual sounds in their language, they learn to put groups of letters together to show words. Then the words go together into sentences. Reading is looking at groups of sentences to get the meaning. This means, in a very important way, reading depends on matching the sounds of spoken words with letters.

Besides comprehension, a major goal of education is teaching reading and spelling. Lots of time, effort, research and money have gone into various methods for teaching reading and spelling. This chapter, instead of looking at different methods, looks at why the seemingly simple task of matching letters and sounds is hard for many people. It also covers what can happen to reading performance when matching up letters and sounds becomes easy.

JOHN

John got his education at a very prestigious and expensive private school in the New England area. He was very successful in football, wrestling, and track. His classmates liked him and his teachers liked his disciplined, hardworking approach to school. John's discipline and hard work were important since that was how, with extra time and special help, he could finish tasks that used reading and spelling.

After eleven years of superb and specialized private school education John was in trouble. It took him too long to do basic reading and writing. It took him so much time to read and spell that John could not qualify to attend the competitive colleges {Yale, Princeton, Stanford, Harvard, etc.}. This was especially frustrating because his parents had paid for private schooling to help be sure John could get into a competitive college.

Testing done the middle of his twelfth grade year showed John could read words from a list at a tenth grade level. He could spell at an eighth grade level. He could figure out words he had never seen before as well as a fourth grader. But, by using context cues, John could read paragraphs at a twelfth grade level.

It might seem, because he could compensate and do twelfth grade level reading, that John really did not need special help. In spite of his grade level context reading, John got into trouble because he was uncertain about how to read and spell so many words. Because he was unsure, it took John a really long time to read new material or write a paper.

The last part of his senior year John spent sixty-one hours in the Lindamood® program. Instead of doing what he had done for the last eleven years, activities that left him unsure in reading and spelling, John did the Lindamood® program steps that help people be aware of the sounds within words. After the sixty-one hours, John read words from a list above a twelfth grade level. He spelled at a twelfth grade level and could figure out words he had never seen before better than an average twelfth grader. John also continued to read in context at a twelfth grade level. Although the help did not come soon enough to let John qualify for a competitive college, he did enter a state college and is having a successful college career.

There are many people who struggle, unsuccessfully, to learn to read and spell as well as they speak. Section 2 gives figures showing as much as thirty-three percent of the United States' population does not learn basic levels of reading and spelling. Interestingly, it is not only sighted people who struggle to learn reading and spelling. There are blind people who struggle to learn to show sounds and words with Braille. This happens even when the different people seem equal in basic intelligence, motivation, and ability.

How is this possible? Is there some ability so basic that it affects reading and spelling whether the person uses visual letters or tactile Braille letters? To help show the range of people who can struggle with reading and spelling let's look at Amanda and Brett.

Amanda

Amanda comes from a wealthy family. By the time she was eight she had already lived in two different countries where she went to private schools and had private tutoring. Amanda was born with, not a silver, but a platinum spoon in her mouth. She had every opportunity and access to every kind of special help.

Amanda lived in a very lively situation. When she was still in second grade, Amanda went to parties where her parents entertained ambassadors and representatives from all over the world. She had spent time with the ambassadors of the USSR, France, Greece, and Britain before she started third grade.

In spite of this enriched environment and the many resources available to her, Amanda was struggling in the U.S. school she was attending for third grade. She had very superior verbal skills and the best kinds of tutorial help money could buy. Unfortunately, from week to week Amanda was unable to spell or read at a level acceptable for a third grader.

BRETT

Brett struggled in school all his life. Although he was not a behavior problem, he was often in the counselor's or principal's offices because he didn't do his school work. In spite of his problems, however, Brett meant to attend college. His family wanted to help Brett go to college since he wanted to do that with his life.

Beginning his sophomore year in high school his counselors told Brett that he was just "not college material." They wanted him to enter vocational and technicaltechnical training. When their talks didn't change Brett's determination to attend college, the counselors brought in his parents. They told his parents that there was no hope for Brett at college. He just didn't have the basic reading and spelling skills he needed to do college level work. The counselors said that if Brett didn't start to learn some vocational and technical skills, he could lose his chances to learn to make a living.

Brett's parents said it was the school's responsibility to educate Brett. That meant teaching him basic reading and spelling skills. In response, his counselors listed off the efforts made to teach Brett reading and spelling over the years. They said the opportunity for Brett to learn those skills had been provided. Most of Brett's classmates had learned to read and spell well enough from the school's efforts, but he had not. Now the school was trying to do its job by guiding Brett into a kind of learning where he could succeed. It was almost certain he would do well in vocational or technical training. The counselors felt it was important for Brett to use the learning opportunity they were trying to arrange.

The issue preventing John, Amanda, and Brett from developing the reading and spelling skills they need is like the issue in Chapter One. It is so evident that, in the past, everybody assumed everybody else did it.

Languages that use symbols, letters, to show sounds are usually called phonetic. With phonetic languages most people assume persons with good hearing have the auditory ability they need to learn reading and spelling. Recent research into hearing and auditory processing {how the brain deals with sound after it's been heard} shows this assumption is incorrect. Research into the ability called auditory processing, phonological processing, phonological awareness, or phoneme segmentation shows that many people have trouble identifying sounds within words once they've heard the word. This research validates the breakthrough of Charles and Patricia Lindamood in their work with the ability of the brain to process sounds within words. The Lindamoods call the ability "auditory conceptualization."

All the terms noted above basically mean a person can tell the individual sounds that make up a word. For example, in the word "map," a person hears the word as a chunk of sound. They can tell it is different from the other words {chunks of sound} in a phrase like "look at the map." In addition, people with fully developed auditory conceptual ability can tell that the one word "map" is made up of only certain sounds, arranged in a specific order. If a person with fully developed auditory conceptual ability saw "map" and read "pam" they would know that they had all the right sounds, but in a wrong order. Knowing this would let them fix their mistake. Persons without fully developed auditory conceptual ability often cannot tell they have even made a reading error unless the word is in their visual memory.

{In the following illustrations readers please be aware the music notes just show the general idea of sound, not specific musical tones of a specific length.}

illustration # 18
In reading we match the letters to sounds, so it is like a
person is speaking to us. Sometimes this process gets
mixed up.

illustration # 19
If your brain sorts the sounds, you can tell there is a mixup.

illustration # 20
Then you can fix the mistake. Most reading and spelling
errors are much easier to fix if your brain can sort out
the sounds in the words.

For some people, trouble sorting the sounds to know they made an error starts with words the size of "map" or "was." For others, trouble starts with words the size of "immigration" or "imagination." Seriously undeveloped auditory conceptual ability can even affect speech. Archie Bunker, from the old television series All in the Family, is an example of someone with very undeveloped auditory conceptual ability.

Since phonetic languages show the sounds in words with letters, reading and spelling are harder for persons who can't tell for sure about the sounds in the words. To read and spell to their potential persons need to be able to tell for sure how many sounds are in a word, exactly which sounds they are, and the exact order of the sounds within the word.

In the past it was assumed a person with good hearing had good auditory conceptual ability. If a person could hear, they could tell what was happening with the sounds inside the words. Auditory conceptual research by pioneers Patricia and Charles Lindamood {and more recently by developmental psychologists, audiology scientists, neuroscientists, and others} uncovered the fact that at least thirty-three percent of the population, with normal hearing ability, does not have fully developed auditory conceptual ability. This means over thirty percent of the population is missing an ability vital to effective reading and spelling. Also, research with the blind has identified that students struggling with reading and spelling in Braille do not have fully developed auditory conceptual ability.

This brings up dyslexia, the word used to describe so many reading and spelling problems. Researcher's keep adding refinements to the term, coining things like "visual dyslexia," or "auditory dyslexia," and even "kinesthetic dyslexia." Usually, and for the purposes of this book, dyslexia means a person who has trouble with reading and spelling for no clear reason. The person is bright, has a good oral vocabulary, may even do well with numbers and math, but reading and spelling are hard. Most people, when they think of dyslexia think; "Oh yeah, that's where the person sees the word backward." Let's think for a minute about what people called "dyslexic" do when they make a reading or spelling mistake. They add sounds to words that don't belong, like spelling or reading a word as "stastistics," instead of statistics. They leave sounds out of words, like reading or spelling the word stream as "steam." They substitute sounds that don't belong in the word for sounds that do belong, like spelling or reading immigration as "imagination." Sometimes they even shift around the order of the sounds in the word, like reading or spelling pam for "map."

Notice that the errors dyslexic's make are errors with the sounds in the word(s). In one clinic, working with people classified as dyslexic for over fifteen years, each dyslexic client saw words clearly. If asked to put a finger under the first letter in the word "saw," the client(s) could put their finger(s) under the s. {If they couldn't do that, their visual-spatial abilities were checked and corrected, but that is in the next chapter}. Asked to move their finger(s) to the second letter, the client(s) moved their finger(s) under the a. And asked to move their finger(s) to the last letter, the client(s) put their finger(s) under the w. They could see the order of the letters correctly, but, when asked to say the word, they often said "was." The problem was not how they saw the word, but how they turned the word into sound. When tested, these clients had slightly to severely undeveloped auditory conceptual ability. With development of their auditory conceptual ability, they stopped adding sounds to words, leaving sounds out of words, and substituting the wrong sounds within words. Basically, they stopped making the reading and spelling mistakes that caused them to be called "dyslexic."

Since developing auditory conceptual ability can help most "dyslexic" people read and spell better, how can this ability be developed? To start, a trained professional helps the person use the sensory information of mouth movement. This additional sensory information, combined with hearing, helps the person verify the specific sounds that make up a word. Thinking about the sounds is organized around the mouth movement that produces the sound, instead of just the alphabet letters.

illustration # 21
Knowing how your mouth moves for the sounds gives a way
for you to verify the sounds in the words.

Once a person knows the mouth movements that produce individual sounds, the movements can be used to track and verify the identity and order of sounds in words. Now, besides just sounds and letters, the person has another way to sort out what makes up a word.

illustration # 22
Now, besides just letters and sounds, you can use mouth
movements to help figure out the parts of a word.

When the sounds in words {syllables} first start to be sorted out, a person shows the mouth feelings that make up that word. First the person shows the feelings with mouth pictures and then colored blocks. Colored blocks are used so the person doesn't have to remember a specific letter, or combination of letters, that show the mouth movement/sound. For instance, if they use a blue block to show the "n" sound and then take out the "n" sound, they can use the blue block to show another sound, like "s" next time. All the person has to do with "map" for example, is show three blocks, each a different color. When they can do that, it shows the person is aware of not only the whole word, but also of the three different sounds that make up "map."

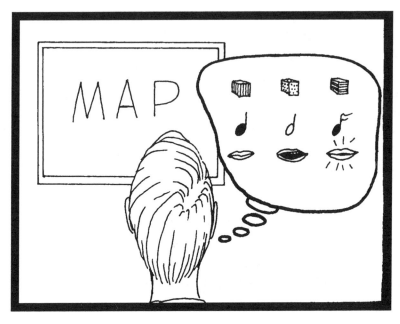

illustration # 23
The blocks let you focus just on sorting out what makes up the word. After that part is easy, using letters is much easier and more logical.

Once the person can tell the mouth movements/sounds in one syllable words, showing this awareness with the blocks, then they move to using letters to show one syllable words. Now is when the regularities and irregularities of written visual symbols are explored. The person can be more successful using the logic of the phonetic reading and spelling system because they can judge which sounds go with which letters. The minor irregularities that must be remembered are much easier to deal with when the person no longer has to try to remember the look of every single word.

illustration # 24
Letters are a natural step once you can judge the
sounds they show.

When a person can deal with one-syllable words successfully, two-syllable words are explored, then three-syllable, four-syllable, and five-syllable words.

As was the case in Chapter One, this is a very simplified explanation. The actual impact of the procedures for developing auditory conceptual ability is still being explored. Research, to date, suggests the procedures

illustration # 25
Using all these levels of awareness makes it possible to
sort out words of almost any length.

stimulate changes in brain function. A more complete explanation of
the procedures, and information about training in them, is available by
contacting the author using the sheet in the Appendix.

What happens when this program is used to develop auditory
conceptual ability?

AMANDA

Amanda successfully completed third grade and went on to operate very successfully in an academically accelerated private school. Her family especially enjoys Amanda's success since her father, aunts, uncles, and grandparents were very aware of the struggles she would have faced in school. Most of them had struggled with reading and spelling problems themselves. It was the family history of learning difficulties that allowed them to spot Amanda's situation and seek help for her early in her school experience.

BRETT

Brett, after going through the program, successfully graduated from high school. He did enroll in college, as was his dream, and earned a Bachelor's degree in the usual four years. In addition this young man, who had been guided away from advanced education, recently finished his Master's degree and is pursuing a Ph.D. at his local university.

Page for

Notes / Comments / Questions

Chapter Three

Drawing and Handwriting

So easy and yet so hard

In modern life dealing with visual-motor and visual-spatial tasks is important. People often deal with papers or computer screens that need to have drawing or writing put on them, or they deal with signs, papers, and computer screens that already have writing and drawing on them. People who easily deal with line and space relationships have an easier time than those who struggle with these relationships. Success with line and space relationships requires visual-spatial and visual-motor ability. Visual-spatial ability lets a person tell things like near and far or up and down, while visual-motor ability lets them draw or move in the space they perceive.

Printing is an early visual-spatial/visual-motor task for students. Printing seems easy and automatic for the experienced student. But, it actually requires many discrete, precise visual judgements, motor acts, and then judgements about the results of those acts.

illustration # 26
Learning visual-motor tasks takes thinking and effort.

Printing or writing are not the only times a student uses visual-spatial/ visual-motor relationships. They learn to form numbers and put the numbers in certain spatial relationships to each other. They also learn to draw maps and diagrams, and to use road and geographic maps. Some students learn to read electronic schematics or computer flow charts. They may learn to draw musical notations, position sewing materials, manipulate tools, or do any of the thousands of other things that use visual-spatial/visual-motor judgements. Just by living in an organized society people constantly need to deal with lines, spaces, and visual symbols.

illustration # 27
We live in a world of visual information; it is all round us.

Developing the ability to make visual-spatial judgements and the visual-motor skills to act on those judgements requires active practice. People who work with motor skills {occupational therapists, sensory integration therapists, and others} have identified that motor activity and visual experiences together help develop visual-spatial/visual-motor ability. A graphic demonstration of the link between motor activity and visual experiences can be found in an experiment done with cats. {Those of you who are curious can get more detailed information about these experiments from almost any neuro-biology college text.} In the experiment cats grew up in a setting with no horizontal lines. Also, they had no motor experience with horizontal planes {other than the single level floor of the experimental chamber}.

Once they were grown the cats were moved to an environment with horizontal lines and planes of different levels. The cats had a hard time in this new environment. They could not jump down from the top of a table to the seat of a chair. They had great difficulty moving up or down a staircase. By missing visual experiences linked with motor experiences, an important part of their full development did not occur. Humans, of course, are not isolated from certain kinds of lines and planes, yet some people don't, on their own, develop the ability to deal successfully with visual-spatial/visual-motor tasks. They need more direct stimulation to become fully independent and functional in these areas.

Besides the convenience of using lines and spaces successfully {like making a quick sketch to give directions}, good visual-motor skills can lower personal stress. Underdeveloped visual-motor performance can cause a person to appear awkward or questionable to their working peers and friends. If a handwritten note is unreadable, or the map to a party is impossible to follow, the person who produced them seems less competent. They may feel stress every time they have to write a note or draw something. Superior visual-motor skills, on the other hand, can enhance a person's standing with their friends and co-workers, as Adam demonstrates.

> While he was in the Navy, Adam used to stand his time as duty officer and make log entries like the other officers. Often his log entries would be word for word the same as the entry of the previous duty officer. But Adam consistently got higher ratings than the other officers for his performance as duty officer. He had learned formal lettering during some training in architectural drafting. This made the appearance of his log entries sharply different from the ones above and below. The difference was so great that, although the content was the same, he was evaluated as a better performer than the other officers.

Often, if a student does not show the expected level of visual-motor performance while they are learning to print, teachers decide they have a delay in visual-motor development. The usual suggestion is to give the child time to grow out of it. If, after growing a bit more, a child still cannot do what is expected, sensory integration or other visual-motor programs may be recommended. After these programs, if there is still no change, parents usually are encouraged to get the child a typewriter or computer. But, when the child grows up, they still have a problem. If a computer or typewriter is not available they appear awkward. Often, whether they want to or not, they have to joke about their "chicken scratching" to cover for their visual-motor difficulties.

MARY

Mary was an almost perfect student. She had above average comprehension and above grade level reading and spelling skills. But Mary had a terrible time learning handwriting and drawing. It was so difficult for her that her parents and the school arranged to have her tested. The test results made clear she had a serious problem in visual-motor activities. She would add extra lines to drawings, leave out necessary lines, and so distort some of her lines that it was hard to tell what she was trying to draw. To help change this situation, Mary went to sensory integration therapy provided by an Occupational Therapist. Much of the treatment focussed on gross motor activities, balancing, spinning and recovering, or performing various tasks while bouncing on a mini-trampoline. Mary went to her therapy sessions for the next school year. End of the year testing revealed showed Mary's marked improvement with gross-motor skills. Unfortunately, Mary made no improvement in the pencil and paper type visual-motor skills she needed for school. Each year for the next two years the school tested Mary's visual-motor performance. Each year Mary made no improvement. Four years after the school recognized her visual-motor difficulties and tried to help, Mary spent three hours in Phyllis Lindamood's *Drawing with Language* program. {The program steps are described later in this chapter.} After the three hours, Mary gained three years on a standard visual-motor test. The next time the school psychologist tested her, after twelve more hours of *Drawing with Language* work, Mary was above her age and grade level in all types of visual-motor performance.

Education recognizes the importance of visual-motor skills. It needs students who can deal with visual-spatial relationships in paper and pencil tasks. As Mary shows, however, there are limits with the help students generally receive when they seem unable to develop such abilities. The support services community {occupational therapists, sensory integration therapists, and others} usually works with very basic levels of visual-motor development. Levels like balance, directionality, and mid-line recognition are so basic that, even when the individual is successful with them, they still have trouble with paper and pencil tasks. As Mary showed, the usual types of help did not enable her to do the visual-motor things needed in her day to day school life.

MARK

Everybody thought Mark's visual-motor problems came from the fact he was legally blind. But, even allowing for his vision problems, Mark was having so much trouble in school that his parents wanted to get him extra help. Just on a trial Mark spent twenty hours in the *Drawing with Language* program. When Mark started the program his visual-motor performance was the same as a child three and a half years old, though he was nine years old. After the twenty hours Mark took some more tests to see if anything was happening. Now his visual-motor performance was the same as a child six and a half years old. In twenty hours Mark gained three years in visual-motor performance. This gain surprised Mark's parents and school officials. They all thought, because of Mark's visual impairments, it was impossible to change his basic visual-motor performance.

In any visual-motor task, whether it is learning to print letters or draw a diagram, most people think they just need to copy what they see. Since most people can copy what they see fairly well, it is often confusing and frustrating when a person cannot seem to learn to copy easily and successfully.

The previous two chapters dealt with other important basic skills some people have trouble learning. A close look at what a person using the basic skill really had to do uncovered some abilities needing more development. After a person developed the necessary ability, their performance improved. A close look at copying, just as in the case of the other basic abilities, reveals hidden complexity in even a "simple" copying task.

Copying something as simple as a printed letter C means a student first has to put the C a certain place. The student has to decide about placing it at the top, to the left, to the right, at the bottom, in the middle, on a line, above a line, between the lines, in blank space, or in relationship to something else on the paper.

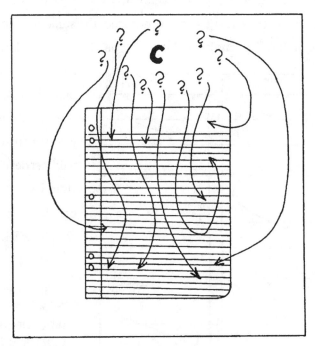

illustration # 28
Visual-motor actions start by picking a place to begin.

After choosing a starting place on the page, the student must pick a starting point for the letter C. As a third step a student must move their pencil tip away from the letter's starting point with a curving line that goes up from the starting point and toward the left side of the page. But, after the curving line has reached a certain point the student must do a fourth step. They must change the line so it begins to go down, while still curving and still heading toward the left side of the paper. At another point the student must do a fifth step by changing the line so it continues down, but curves toward the right side of the page. A sixth step is to change the line so it begins to curve up while it goes toward the right side of the page. Finally, as a seventh step, the student must select an ending point. The ending point has to have a specific relationship to the starting point. In order for a student to do the seemingly simple job of copying a C, a whole series of carefully timed steps must be quickly done in a certain order.

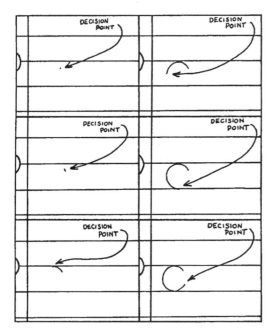

illustration # 29
A look at all of the other decisions that have to be made just to copy a letter C.

Recognizing the complexities involved in visual-motor performance, Phyllis Lindamood's program makes few assumptions about a person's starting ability. The first steps in the Drawing with Language program deal with basic ideas of distance and direction. The first steps help the person make decisions about things like near and far or up and down. The early steps also help the person learn to judge these things when a surface is flat on a table or up on a wall. The other critical thing the early steps teach is how to describe these, and other, visual-motor/visual-spatial issues with language.

Once distance and direction judgments are reliable, the person learns the units they will need to draw and write, lines and points. Lines can be straight, curved, vertical, horizontal, or diagonal. The first step in producing a line is picking a starting point. Starting points are important because placement of the starting point can make any drawing much easier or much harder. Starting points, ending points, and lines are first learned using manipulatives to help demonstrate, in a concrete way various concepts. Manipulatives make it easier to grasp something like, "a starting point in the left center of the page with a downward curving line that has an ending point in the right center part of the page." When the person is able to produce starting points, various kinds of lines, and ending points anywhere on a page, the move is made to drawing without the manipulatives. In keeping with the major premise of Phyllis's Drawing with Language program, however, language is still used.

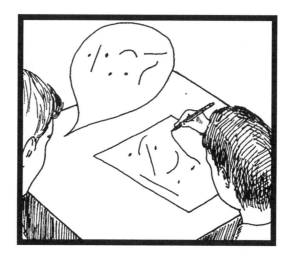

illustration # 30
First comes learning the basic parts that make up visual-motor
activity and how language enables you to use the basic units
of visual-motor expression, lines and points.

People practice by putting the basic units on paper using language
directions, instead of right away trying to copy figures and/or objects.
Once working with language and the basic units is reliable, the next
step is drawing. At this point, instead of only working with lines and
points, the person begins to put one, then two, then three, and then
four or more lines together, eventually learning about shapes. {For
example, four straight lines in a certain relationship to each other make
a square, but in another relationship the lines make a rectangle. Or
three lines with certain starting and ending points make an equilateral
triangle, while the same three lines with different starting and ending
points combine to create an isosceles triangle}.

illustration # 31
Language is used to help you put the lines and points into shapes.

After persons can draw basic shapes and position them in specific places on the page {like the middle left area of the paper}, language helps them combine the basic shapes into figures.

Figure drawing has the person use their ability to think with shapes and positions to create objects. Instead of just drawing a shape, the focus is on making the basic shapes and lines combine to create a figure that looks like something from real life.

For example, a person looks at a bike and describes the main features: two big circles side by side, etc. They describe and draw the different lines and various shapes they see until they have produced the figure of a bicycle.

illustration # 32
Drawing a figure of something from every day life can just
mean combining basic shapes, points, and lines.

As with the other two programs, this is a very simplified description. The program extends into organized work on the page, print/cursive writing, maps, 3-D drawing, etc. Just like the other two programs, learning the basic units and how to think and talk about them makes a profound difference. Thinking about and being able to describe the basic units seems so, well, basic, that usually no one checks to see if a person really can detect and talk about them. Mary and Mark show there are people who are unaware of the basic units of visual-motor performance. They also show what is possible when someone is helped to connect language with sensory experience by a professionally trained person. The value of good visual-motor abilities is best described by the phrase "one picture is worth a thousand words." Having the visual-motor skills that allow good handwriting and that allow quick and accurate drawing can be very valuable and life enriching.

illustration # 33
Good visual-motor and visual-spatial skills can make life easier, more fun, and more successful.

Page for
Notes / Comments / Questions

Chapter Four

Learning

What can happen when people can learn

Two people were talking about the {at that time} recent discovery of electricity. The first person said, "Yes, it may be interesting, but what good is it?" The other replied, "What good is a new born baby?"

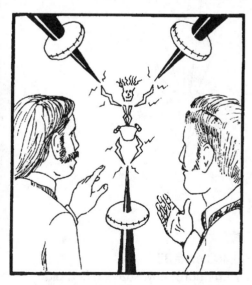

illustration # 34
When electricity was new, in other words a baby, few people had any idea it would develop, grow up, into something of value in the real world of day to day life.

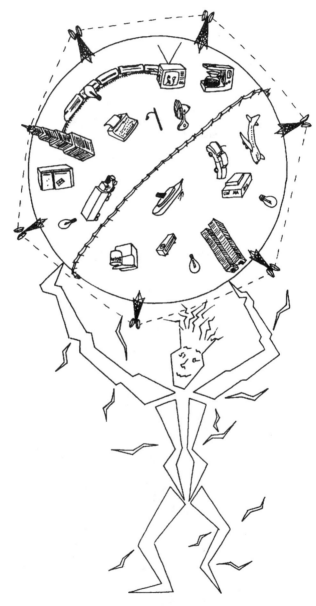

illustration # 35
Electricity is not a baby anymore, nowadays it is a giant.

All of us in the present find our lives profoundly changed by electricity. That useless scientific curiosity of the past has completely altered our way of life. It is the foundation for changes still transforming our world. Electricity powers a telephone network that lets us punch some numbers and talk with a person next door, or on the other side of the planet. It powers computers that are remaking the ways we live and work. It is in our towns and homes powering televisions, movies, machines, pumps, lights, and starting cars. If electricity, as we know it, were removed from the earth — life, as we know it, would end. Phones and computers would stop working. Skyscrapers, that need electricity for air circulation, elevators, and lighting, would be empty and useless. Airlines, that need electricity for navigation, radar, and hundreds of other things, would be grounded. Cars, that need electricity to start and provide the spark that burns the fuel, would stop. Electricity, a useless new born child in history, has grown up to carry almost an entire world on its back.

The programs covered in the earlier chapters are also new born babies. There is evidence they may grow up to change the world as deeply as has electricity.

People who study the future point out there is a knowledge explosion. There is now more to know, in the way of factual knowledge, than ever before in history. Also the amount of factual knowledge is growing like a magic penny. {A penny that doubles itself, first you have one, then two, then four, eight, sixteen, thirty five, two, sixty four, etc.}. Confronted with this growing heap of information, society tries to reward people who are good at learning. In modern business, people who can speak two languages generally move ahead faster than persons who speak only one. The people who can adapt, adjust, and keep up with new developments, tend to be the people most richly rewarded by their society.

In the past education was a privilege only for the wealthy. In the present education is a necessity for all people. In the future anything that can profoundly increase success in learning, and thereby success in education, will be vital. The programs in the earlier chapters are some of the most important breakthroughs for learning and education since the development of writing and the printing press. When used correctly, these programs improve, sometimes dramatically, the ability of a person to learn and, consequently, to succeed in education.

Most evidence for the potential of these programs comes from individual case histories. There are now thousands of individual case histories. They all verify the experiences of the people from earlier chapters. The programs are too new to have been studied and tested on a society wide scale. But, their possible value can be predicted from the individual experiences available and the few larger scale studies done to date.

NanciBell®'s program for developing language comprehension is very important. There is almost no part of life untouched by language. Several professions like law, politics, advertising, counseling, and teaching use language as the main basis for their work. Language is part of almost every aspect of life for the people and institutions that make up a society.

Below are a few examples of how issues of language comprehension can change lives.

A project in a maximum security facility for the criminally insane identified several problem inmates. These inmates would say, in group therapy, that they were going to do certain things and then they would not do those things, or do just the opposite. The inmates would have certain jobs and fail to do the job. As part of the project the inmates went through some testing. This testing uncovered that these problem inmates had the same memory for oral directions as three to eight year old children. They had the same grasp of cause and effect relationships as children six to ten years old. They had the general oral language comprehension of persons less than twelve years old.

illustration # 36
The inmates did not have the necessary
language processing abilities.

These twenty-five to thirty-eight year old men were in treatment groups run by workers who assumed the men had twenty-five to thirty-eight year old language abilities. In group therapy the inmates could parrot the right words and guess what to say by nonverbal cues {if the group leader leans their head forward and to the left you should agree, etc.}. They seemed completely sincere when they committed themselves to new behaviors. But, most of the time they really did not remember, or did not understand, these commitments. So, moments after the group session ended, they would often do a behavior they had agreed to change.

Valarie, from Chapter One, and her husband went to three different counseling psychologists to try to work on their marriage. They tried to get help, but the help didn't work for them. The counselors thought the problem was motivation or communication. When their efforts to help in these areas did not work, the counselors dismissed their failure by deciding Valarie was a resistant client. They thought, if she really wanted to change and save her marriage she would do the things discussed, with language, in the sessions. The real problem was, of course, that Valarie did not understand the language used in the sessions.

Jenny, also from Chapter 1, was a problem child. She seemed like a person who was able, but just unwilling to try. A student who just needed to have a fire lit under her in order for her to pay attention and do her work. When all the fire lighting efforts did not work, her failures were dismissed with the decision that Jenny was a kid bent on failure. Everyone decided nothing could be done about it unless she would motivate herself.

These examples are not to say that all people in prison, in therapy, or with school problems have a language comprehension problem. It is to say that many of these people probably do have some kind of learning problem and one of the first things to check is their ability to understand and interpret language.

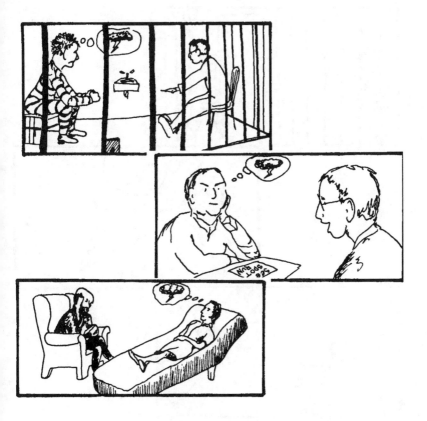

illustration # 37
Many people getting help cannot comprehend the words
of the people trying to help them.

If they could learn successfully, or truly understand the language being used around them, how many would stay in prison, therapy, or special school programs because they really like it? Based on experiences with hundreds of individuals, checking comprehension will help the professionals involved work more effectively with most of them.

illustration # 38
Once they can comprehend the words used by those trying to help, many respond successfully and change their lives.

The potential impact of the Lindamood® auditory conceptual developments is also tremendous. Mental health professionals link a loss of self esteem to the start of many other kinds of mental and behavior problems. Untold numbers of people have their self esteem crippled by failure in reading and spelling. Their friends and classmates learn to read and spell easily, but it is hard for them. Their friends and classmates talk about a "dumb" kid who reads like a baby and they read the same way as the "dumb" kid. In a little while these individuals get self esteem problems. From when they were O.K. about school, these people come to a point when they are sick morning after morning of the school year. Problems can grow from this beginning until their reading difficulty seems unimportant compared to the other problems {drugs, behavior, etc.} in their lives.

Beyond their personal impact, the Lindamood® program and test have great promise for education. In the 1970's a small town in the U.S. state of Idaho started using the Lindamood® program with their first grade students. Several years later the program showed this striking result. Second to fifth graders from 1971 to 1974, who had not had Lindamood® work in first grade, got an average reading score at the 52nd percentile. {The scores were on the Iowa Tests of Basic Skills [ITBS].} Second to fifth graders from 1975 to 1979, who had had Lindamood® work in first grade, got an average reading score at the 86th percentile on the ITBS. {Figure #1, next page, shows these numbers.}

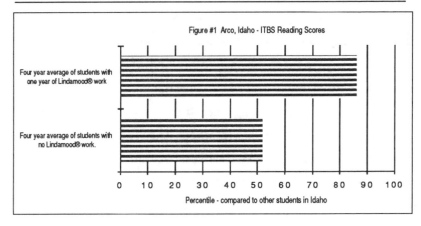

Figure #1 Arco, Idaho - ITBS Reading Scores

In the 1980's a small town in the U.S. state of California started using the Lindamood® program with their kindergarten through second grade students. Testing at the start of the project showed no significant differences between the students in classes that were going to use the Lindamood® procedures and the students in classes that were not going to use the procedures. By the end of the year the classes that had Lindamood® work were significantly superior to the other classes in all the areas tested. When two kindergarten classes went to first grade, with the one class continuing their Lindamood® work, the class getting Lindamood® got even farther ahead of the other class. By the end of first grade students in the Lindamood® class gained a mean of 4.7 years in word attack. {Word attack is the ability to figure out how to read new words. This skill is very helpful to first graders since they constantly run into new words in their reading.} The other class gained a mean of .58 years in word attack ability. {See Figure #2 on the next page for a chart of these numbers.}

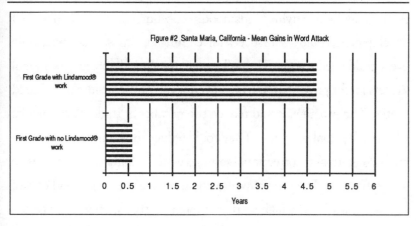

Figure #2 Santa Maria, California - Mean Gains in Word Attack

When a class with two years of Lindamood® work got to third grade, school district testing revealed some unusual results. None of the students were below average on the Word Study Skills or Spelling Structural Principles subtests of the Stanford Achievement Test. They were the only third grade class, out of four in their school, with no students below average on these two subtests. Also, their National Group Stanine rank was superior. They were the only third grade in their school with superior rank, though a different third grade class had all the students classified as "gifted" in it.

These two studies, and others, show that the Lindamood® procedures can nearly eliminate most of the reading and spelling problems now so troublesome in the United States. Use of the Lindamood® procedures with the Nancibell® procedures might eliminate most of the learning disabled students in the United States. Use of these procedures in the early grades, with Phyllis Lindamood's procedures for visual conceptual development, could assure successful learning for almost every practically every child in education. The dollar savings such widespread educational success might provide is startling, even if you only consider the United States. The programs could reduce the number of students and adults who need special programs. They could reduce the number of people in mental health and correctional services while helping these services be more effective. The programs also could reduce the length and cost of retraining workers by making them more effective learners. The global impact from widespread recognition and use of these methods is almost beyond calculation.

Besides the dollar values these programs offer, there are human values more difficult to measure in numbers. One client put it this way:

> *"You lose a lot. You don't have self esteem. You're always walking around very self conscious. You don't put yourself out in a position to go for that advancement at your job. You sit there and you say 'I can't do it because I can't spell' {or read, or understand}, so it keeps you quiet. It took me four hours a day, five days a week, for four weeks. That's really nothing when you realize that I've been this way all my life. And when do you start going to school? When you're six or seven you start learning the basic skills and I'm forty three years old now, . . . I wish that I had done this a lot sooner."*

illustration # 39
If students have the basic abilities they need, they can
move through education to achieve whatever they wish
with their lives. Educational success rests on certain
basic abilities.

Page for

Notes / Comments / Questions

Chapter Five

Questions and Answers
What people often ask

Below are questions that have come up in discussions and training events. They may answer your questions but, if you still have some, see the Appendix.

If these methods are so great, why don't more people know about them?

The programs are fairly new. It usually takes quite awhile for information on something new, that is not a movie or fashion item hyped by the media, to spread.

Another issue is the amount of time it takes to train people. A professional doing one of the programs must learn both a body of information and certain procedures for interacting with the client or student. The information can be taught in a normal style training event. The interaction procedures, however, need a type of apprenticeship that takes time and supervision. For now the methods cannot spread too rapidly because only a handful of experienced people are available to train others. It generally takes two to four years of closely supervised work for someone to become competent and fully effective with these programs. It takes an additional two to four years of work for them to become competent to support others learning to use the programs.

Another slowing factor is that the programs are, for now, very labor intensive. The people getting the extended training described above can help about twenty clients a year. A carefully developed clinical operation can treat up to two hundred clients a year. But, it takes several years to develop the pool of trained staff needed to deal with this larger number of clients.

If these programs take so much training and are so labor intensive, can they be much use in the real world?

Yes, especially in view of the cost of not using them. Plus, used preventively, like the Chapter Four school projects, the procedures can be done with groups instead of the one-to-one settings needed with individuals beyond second grade.

Technology also may help. Interactive multimedia may be able to lessen the length of training and increase the number of clients served by a trained individual. Pilot efforts to develop multimedia resources are underway. If the resources are successful they will greatly enhance the availability of these programs.

Many of the people talked about earlier did not seem to have really serious problems, are the programs useful with hard-core learning problems?

The programs developed in private clinics. This means people coming for services paid for it out of their own pockets, beyond the dollars taxed out of their pockets and given to schools. Because the people coming for help had to pay, they usually tried every other kind of help first.

Using the programs, high school graduates, with bona fide diploma's, who did not know the alphabet, have learned to read and write. College students, who were making it in college by having their husbands, wives, or close friends read their books to them, write their papers for them, and help them memorize possible test questions, have become independent and successful in college. In a few, very unusual, cases people identified as retarded have been able to move on into average school work.

The programs are, simply, one of the most productive things that can be done with a person who has a learning problem the programs address. They can also enhance the learning of those without learning problems.

If the help these programs give is really so vital, how can 33 percent of the adult population, who, according to the statistics, need help, already be teachers, doctors, lawyers, and business people?

The programs have almost nothing to do with intelligence, only with learning performance. For example, if you do not have auditory conceptual ability, so you can easily use phonics, you use visual memory and oral language cues to read and spell. These other methods let you function with reading and spelling. But, also using phonics lets you read and spell more effectively.

People can compensate for missing what these programs help develop, but that is what they are always doing, compensating. They always have to put out extra effort and limit themselves in certain activities. Adults who get help are usually smart and able, they just need more development in one, or all, of these basic abilities to live as independently and confidently as they want to live.

How long does it take to go through a program?

The only way to answer that is with "it depends." Individual situations vary so much that there is no fixed number of sessions or fixed period of service. An average range, how long it usually takes most people, goes like this:

Comprehension development - 80 to 120 hours

Auditory Conceptual development - 100 to 150 hours

Visual motor development - 30 to 60 hours

These estimates are based on services being done in a one to one setting. The estimates assume the person giving the service is specifically trained in these programs. They also assume the hours of work are arranged so a client is getting <u>not less than twenty hours of service a month</u>. Many individuals finish much more rapidly, in only twenty to sixty hours, while some people spend much longer, one hundred seventy five to two hundred fifty hours. It is not possible to predict how long it will actually take for any certain person to complete a program.

How can I tell if somebody might need help?

To know for certain you need to have testing done by a professional trained in the programs.

If you want to know whether the testing is likely to find a need for further help, see if any of the actions of the person you are thinking about match the actions of any of the people you have met through this book.

For comprehension needs, you also can check items like:

a) does the person ask the same type of question over and over again;

b) can the person tell you details about something, but not tell you the main idea;

c) can the person tell you the main idea of something, but not tell you the important details;

d) does the person's conversation seem to lack reasonable order;

e) does the person miss fairly obvious cause-effect connections?

For auditory conceptual needs, you can check items like:

a) when the person misspells a word, is it possible for you to still tell what the word is meant to be, {action spelled with these letters "akshun" is at least phonetically reasonable, spelled "catnio" it is not phonetically reasonable and the person probably needs help};

b) does their handwriting usually run together so it is hard to tell if they mean an E or an I, an A or an O, etc.;

c) how consistently and skillfully does the person avoid situations where they need to spell or read;

d) when they misread a word, is the reading error close or is it way off;

e) in a new part of town, or on vacation, how do they do with the street signs?

For visual conceptual needs, you might check items like:

a) can they at least sometimes do legible printing or handwriting;

b) how easily can they draw a basic shape {triangles, rectangles, or circles};

c) how easily can they tell you what needs to be done to draw a basic shape;

d) how much do you have to help them position a letter or a symbol at a certain spot on the page?

If you find that the person you are thinking about has an unreasonable amount of difficulty with any of the items above, then testing is a good next step. How to decide just what is an "unreasonable" amount of difficulty is a judgement you must make. It may please you to know, however, that most people have pretty good instincts about what is "unreasonable."

How do I tell if the person doing the program with me {or my child} knows what they are doing?

There is no piece of paper or list of "good" people that can tell you who is and who is not competent. Even programs as carefully and vigorously managed as medical training turn out surgeons who do great work and surgeons who do poor work.

A few things that may tell you to look for another person to help you {or your child} are:

a) Is the work you are being asked to do frustrating you? Competent professionals may challenge you, but you should not find yourself seriously frustrated.

b) Is the professional willing to work with you once or twice a week as the only program activity you will have? If so, they do not understand the programs and you should look somewhere else for help.

c) Is the professional also trying to get you to do tutoring kinds of activities {reading, writing papers, school work, etc.}?

These kind of activities are the concluding steps for the programs and should only be done when you are on your last sessions.

d) Is the work boring? The programs, competently done, are almost never boring to the one getting help.

Finally, you must depend on yourself. Are you getting better at comprehending, reading and spelling, or writing and drawing? You can tell if you are learning. If you are not learning, and you go day after day and do what you are asked to do, you should look somewhere else for help.

Does everybody who finishes these programs do great in school?

No. There are many issues to learning and doing well in education. If you comprehend what you read, but don't read an assignment, you do as badly on a test as someone who cannot comprehend what they read.

These programs are important because many of the people having trouble in school are labelled as having an attitude problem, a concentration problem, a vision problem, or who knows what kind of problem. Research shows that most of the people having problems in school need more development of one, or all, of the basic abilities these programs address. With their enhanced abilities most people go on to do better in education. Some people, even when they have fully developed abilities, do not use their new abilities and do not improve in school. Other people, even with fully developed abilities, have other problems that interfere with their school performance.

Do these programs cure dyslexia?

Yes. Just as discussed in Chapter 2, scientists and educators have various definitions for dyslexia. In general the term dyslexia means to have trouble learning to read and spell for no clear reason. People classified as dyslexic are usually of average to above average intelligence. They can successfully use the spoken language. They have no severe emotional or behavioral problems to interfere with their learning. They just have trouble learning to read and spell. To date, everyone classified as dyslexic when they started an appropriate program stopped {by the time they finished and utilized the abilities developed in the program} making the kinds of mistakes that caused them to be classified as dyslexic.

It looks like these programs can help with reading and writing, what about arithmetic?

There is a program in development to help students with math and arithmetic problems. Because this program is still in development it is not generally available. When it is generally known available, it will have it's own chapter in a revised version of this book.

I hope you have enjoyed this look at three exciting new programs. They are a quantum leap for education. I urge you to act on what you have learned from your reading. If you will act, even by doing something as simple as sharing what you have read, you will enrich your life and/or the lives of at least three out every ten people you know. People who struggle with learning are out there, close to you, but this can change through the accurate recognition of their problem and use of an appropriate program to help them.

Page for
Notes / Comments / Questions
on Section One

Section Two

Education

Our short look at the programs in Section One shows they can greatly improve the results of educational effort. This section is a look at education and its goals. If education is doing its job, then the programs in Section One are just interesting developments. If, on the other hand, education is not completely doing its job, these programs are very important breakthroughs.

Figure 1 helps show a general view of issues that contribute to educational success. It shows that many issues, beyond classroom activities, are important to educational success.

Figure 1
Issues that Aid Educational Success

O Medical Supports
   - Basic Health
   - Adequate Vision
   - Adequate Hearing
   - Adequate Visual - Motor Coordination
   - Adequate Ability to Attend

O Tutorial Supports
   - Specific Skills help
   - Specific Content help

Some issues concern the medical sciences. Students regularly take tests during their developing years. The tests attempt to make sure the students have adequate vision, hearing, and motor development. The biggest need for these abilities is clear and such testing is supported by education. If a student has a problem with vision, hearing, or motor action they get services from people in the medical community. Also, a student who needs medical support can get special teaching situations. Education tries to be sure persons with medical impairments still get a chance to learn basic reading, spelling, and number skills.

Another issue education recognizes is the need for tutorial help for students. Because modern education's mandate covers such a wide range of people, there are limits on its ability to deal with all the different students. Some students just need extra time, or extra help, to master new content. Other students need help to learn specific skills for studying, note taking, or general organization. Since education recognizes there are students who need help learning these skills, or extra help mastering certain content, educators usually know some outside tutorial services. Sometimes these outside services are given by teachers from the education system. Other times, people outside any formal education institution provide tutorial support to students.

Figure 2 {on the next page} shows where the programs from Section One fit. These programs come between the medical services and the tutorial services. The programs are both sensory and cognitive in nature. They stimulate sensory abilities, relating to medical services. They also deal with cognitive abilities, relating to the work provided by tutorial support services.

Figure 2
Issues that Aid Educational Success

○ Medical Supports
- Basic Health
- Adequate Vision
- Adequate Hearing
- Adequate Visual - Motor Coordination
- Adequate Ability to Attend

○ Section One Learning Programs

- Concept Imagery -
  comprehending language through
  visualiziing and verbalizing
- Auditory Conceptualization -
  perceiving the identities, order, and
  number of sounds in words
- Visual Conceptualization
  processing visual units used to form
  letters, shapes, or figures

○ Tutorial Supports

- Specific Skills help -
- Specific Content help -

The following chapters will discuss the world of education in general. There will be a short look at education's basic goals and methods and a look at education in the United States. In these chapters there will also be some discussion of the impact the programs from Section One could have when the regular methods of education aren't enough.

Chapter Six

The Educational World

Education is really two worlds

Education really has two worlds. One world is familiar. It is pupils spending time with each other and their teachers. With this familiar world comes a less familiar world of big business and institutional life. A look at both the worlds of education can reveal pressures that help separate education from learning.

Most cultures see education's pupils as their future. Whether it is a tribe, or a nation of huge institutions, both know their ongoing life depends on the children growing up. To insure that the growing children

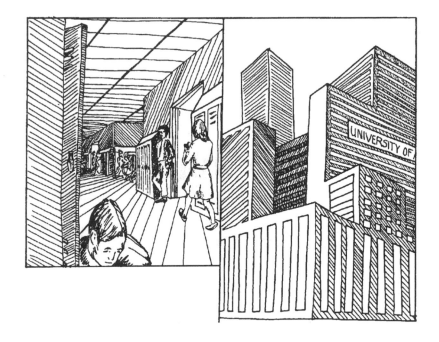

illustration # 40
The two worlds of education: school rooms and big business.

carry on the life of the culture correctly, the children are taught certain facts and to think certain ways. Also various growth experiences are arranged for the children. To achieve these ends and continue their cultural existence, most societies use some kind of education system. Activities in the education system help a child learn what they will need to help them succeed in the next stage of education. In the end, their education helps the child function in their society. In other words, students learn basic steps so they can go to the advanced steps and then move on to sustain the life of their culture.

Education is "human resource development" for a culture. If a culture does not educate its children the culture changes drastically or vanishes. This fact puts the commitment to some form of education at the heart of every society. The commitment is very strong in cultures with institutions. These cultures need people with certain minimum skills. People with minimum skills are so important that banks buy school bonds and provide education loans. Businesses give educational institutions discounts, loan them personnel, and even give money to certain programs. Some large corporations even create their own schools and systems of education. Ultimately, all political and social systems commit major resources to education.

illustration # 41
The big business side of education
struggles for a share of resources.

A result of this major commitment is that education itself becomes an institution. Once it is an institution, education competes with other institutions for dollars, for space, and for personnel.

Besides the outer pressures with other institutions, size also creates internal pressures. A large structure means there are upper and lower

illustration # 42
Institutional educational gives different rewards
at different levels.

level jobs. Different job levels create competition within the education institution for rank, resources, and recognition.

The education institution can become so large that teachers, the ones who share knowledge with the pupils, become minor members. The institution develops its own life. Members can have goals other than teaching students. For example, heads of universities and presidents of colleges spend little, if any, of their time teaching students. They spend most of their time on political, economic, and social aspects of life in the institution. They also spend their time raising money for the school or community awareness of the school. Within institutions, leaders support those who support them. Whether the supporter is a "good" teacher or not can become less important. These issues are all far removed from education's job to pass on the cultural identity and teach the rising generation necessary skills.

Education institutions become concentrations of wealth and power. They are such a part of society that their economic and political power is often not clear beneath the picture of school house, students, teachers, and learning. They generally do not have overt wealth and power like military or government institutions. Education institutions hold a more subtle power and wealth. In tribes, for example, education and religion may be closely tied. People with religious knowledge need to teach that knowledge to others. That means those with the special knowledge can exert considerable influence. They often help select who gets to learn the knowledge and how much they get to learn. The community usually supports the "educators" because they ensure that the rising generation learns the right way to define the world and continue the life of the culture.

In institutional societies, a large use for local and national tax dollars is education. Tax dollars are given directly to education institutions. They are also given through tax exemptions and other benefits. Education institutions also come to control enormous resources in the form of land, buildings, patents, personnel, and even political influence.

illustration # 43
The "little red school house" often controls amazing resources.

Beyond size and dollar issues, another factor, besides teaching, that consumes education's energy is personnel. An education system must have people who teach. The teacher may be a parent, an elder of the tribe, or a formally trained professional. In each of these situations the teacher is to provide knowledge. Teachers need to know more than their pupils and share their knowledge through socially approved methods.

Teachers sharing knowledge, from how to make an arrow to how to launch a space ship, means there are Haves {the teachers} and Have-nots {the students}. Teachers hold a kind of power by being the Haves.

illustration # 44
Education is so important that it is watched and regulated.

This often causes a society to regulate who can teach and what they can teach.

In some tribes, for example, the teaching of young men can only be done by old men. In some nations, teachers can only teach certain ideas and certain parts of history. In other nations teachers need to present samples of all the ideas available in the culture. Consistently, society regulates, formally or informally, who teaches and what is taught. This regulation creates additional dynamics to influence the education system.

All the different dynamics noted in this chapter work to generate pressures that can separate education and learning. They also create a situation that makes institutional education go for the numbers.

o

Chapter Seven

Numbers

Doing it by the numbers - for the numbers

The value of an educated general population creates a rule of numbers. A look into a school room will show anywhere from three to three hundred people. Since everyone is unique, each individual is different from every other individual in the room. But education has the job to be sure these unique individuals finish with the same basic knowledge and abilities {reading, writing, arithmetic, etc.}.

This situation forces education to try to "homogenize" the individuals under its sway. This does not say education fails to see the unique nature of each single individual. Education will teach subjects as different as music, biology, computers, art, medicine, or history in its willingness to support individual abilities and interests. But education's mandate requires that every individual learn certain basic skills despite their abilities or interests. The mandate to teach everyone the basic skills forces education to act as a large scale homogenizer.

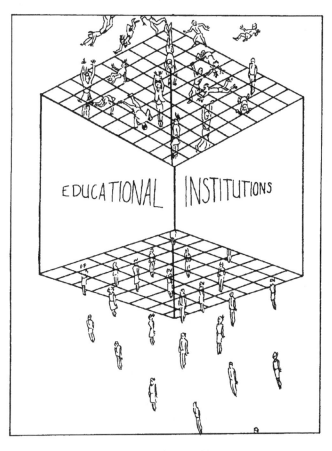

illustration # 45
Education must process students

Picture in your mind's eye a bottle of clear glass filled with milk fresh from a cow. If the bottle is left standing long enough the milk will separate into layers. Thick white cream will go to the top of the bottle and a watery, slightly cloudy, liquid will stay to the bottom. After it has separated, if you pour the contents out into a cup, you do not get your usual cup of milk. You have either a cup of cream or a cup of skim milk.

This type of separation is what education systems are to avoid when teaching the basic skills. If an education system takes a rising generation and turns out too many who do not know the basics, society attacks the education system. If an education system fails to work with everyone, at least at a basic level, those who supply resources to education end their support.

Just as fresh milk is homogenized into groupings, like skim milk or whole milk, education has to process students into groupings by their success in or amount of learning. Also, education has to make sure all students end up in, at least, a basic {skim milk} grouping.

The mandate to deal with so many individuals forces educators to do a lot of defining. They have to define their population and what is reasonable to expect from this population. Their population can be all the people in a society from six years old to eighteen years old. It can also be people of all ages in various college systems. Beyond defining who they work with and what to expect from them, educators must make sure their society knows and accepts the definitions.

All education systems recognize at least two basics every student needs. The first basic is learning to read and spell the written language of their society. Most written languages are phonetic. Generally, phonetic means the letters of the written language represent the sounds of the spoken language. This makes learning written ways to show sounds the first job for most students. In other words, their first job is learning the alphabet. Once students know the alphabet letters that show the sounds of their language, they learn to use groups of alphabet letters to show words. Soon, when they read a line of print it is just as if someone were speaking to them.

The second basic is numbers. Societies have a number system to describe what language cannot easily describe. If a person wants to build a room and goes to a builder saying, "I want you to build me a big room," the builder may not know what the person means. Numbers define clearly what the person means by the words "a big room." If a person says, "I'll give you a puppy for some money," numbers clearly define "some." Students first learn the individual numbers and order of those numbers. From this beginning, they learn to use numbers for describing shapes, spaces, amounts of money, and all the other things numbers do.

Once students have enough of the basics, education goes on to teach them the other knowledge they need. This advanced education often involves history, the society's political and economic system, and other special bodies of knowledge. When students know the basics, education can recognize and support their individual abilities by teaching them almost any additional knowledge they may wish to learn.

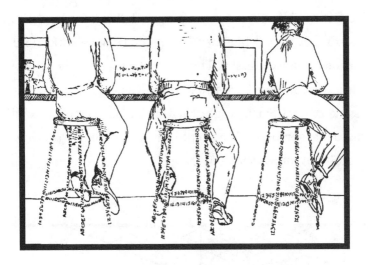

illustration # 46
Future learning rests on the foundation of basic skills.

For instance, students may learn how to teach and, themselves, join the education system. Some students learn to use numbers to describe what happens with molecules and enter atomic or genetic research. Some learn to draw and go on to design buildings, ships, or airplanes. Or students learn how to direct the activities of complex machines. Institutional societies usually need millions of people equipped with thousands of different different bodies of knowledge. This need means education provides a vital service for the society.

Every student needs the two basics to move on to other, advanced, education. This fact creates great pressure for educational institutions. It means they must define the time, methods, and abilities needed for someone to learn the basics. They also have to define the level of basic skills a student must have before the student can move to the next educational level. Finally, educational institutions must organize all these steps so that appropriately equipped, or "homogenized," students move smoothly out into society.

illustration # 47
Education helps supply society with trained personnel.

Since most future education relies on the basic skills, nearly all education systems, as mentioned above, start by teaching them. When teaching reading and spelling spelling most education systems use the fact that their written language shows their spoken language. They teach reading and spelling with phonics. Pupils drill until they learn the sounds that go with the different letters. The letters are then grouped into words, longer words, and then into sentences. At this point students are reading, spelling, and moving on through the other steps involved in education.

But, educators noticed some students had trouble with phonics. They also noticed that many students who knew phonics didn't use that knowledge to sound their way through all words. Sometimes a student looked at a word, recognized it, and read it. With these observations, educators made another effort to be sure all students learned basic spelling and reading. They started teaching these skills with "sight word" or "look-say" methods. Instead of thinking about what sound goes with which letter, pupils read and spelled by how the words looked.

But some students still had trouble, even using both the "look-say" and the phonics methods. So educators looked again at reading and spelling. This time they noticed many of the pupils struggling with phonics and "look-say" used words talking that they could not read or spell. This observation led to another way of teaching called "psycho-linguistics" or the "whole language" method. Using this method in reading, students predict upcoming words using their spoken language ability. For example, pupils read materials with words left out of them.

Their job is to decide what word goes in the space. For example, a sentence might say "the _____ was in the doghouse." The student predicts the word "dog" to go in the blank.

All of these ways of teaching reading and spelling helped some students do better. Unfortunately, many students still did not learn enough of the basic skills of reading and spelling to advance, successfully, to other educational levels and out into society.

To help the percentage of students still failing, education tried another approach. This approach says reading and spelling are really a combination of all the other methods. So this approach uses an eclectic method. In other words, the students learn reading and spelling according to whatever method, or combination of methods, allow them to learn successfully. Some approaches try to identify and use a student's learning style, or their learning strengths. Other eclectic approaches try to correct a student's learning weaknesses.

But, even with their variety of specific activities, the eclectic methods still fail to help some students succeed with spelling and reading. Because some people still fail, despite all the different methods used to teach them, education developed labels to define these people. Terms like learning disabled, dyslexic, or attention deficit disordered are some terms that describe these individuals. Education works with these pupils because of the mandate it has from society. Except the educational institutions are less responsible if such students fail to have adequate reading and spelling skills when they finish their time in education.

The effort and creativity invested in teaching reading and spelling has also been invested in teaching numbers and math. Arithmetic teaching is usually based around one of three schools of thought. A first school of thought is that students do best by developing a big picture about numbers. Students learn things like the history of numbers, the way numbers relate to each other, and the base system for the numbers. Once they have the "big picture," students spend their time drilling on the basic operations of arithmetic {adding, subtracting, multiplying, etc.} and how to use them.

Another school of thought is based on the idea that students learn about numbers by concrete experience. Pupils learn by manipulating concrete objects and experiencing how the numbers describe what they are doing. Students learning with this school of thought move cubes, rods, or other objects according to the numbers and the arithmetic operations. This helps them see how numbers describe things.

A third school of thought focuses on only teaching the operations. Students learn to add, subtract, multiply, divide, do fractions, etc., by rote memorization of the operational steps. In this school of thought little attention is given to the big picture or concrete experience. Students do drills to memorize what step to do first, second, third, fourth, until they can do any arithmetic operation required in their school situation.

In the United States many different math programs are in use. In the late 1960's and early 1970's a push for "new math," using the big picture school of thought, went through the United States. The results of this effort were mixed and did not insure education fulfilled its mission to provide the number basics for everybody. So, in recent times, the United States has no single school of thought influencing or defining its math instruction programs.

Another basic, besides reading, writing, and arithmetic that is one of education's responsibilities is language comprehension. Implicit in its mandate is education's duty to insure the development of comprehension. In the past education relied on the idea that if a student knew the meaning of each individual word, the student comprehended a sentence. After all, a sentence was just some individual words strung together. As Chapter One showed, this system is not working for many students. A brief excerpt from a newspaper article, released a few years ago, helps show education's current struggles with students who have comprehension problems.

Ninth-grader Jennie jiggled her leg nervously as reading specialist Marvin Cohn asked her to read a paragraph any fourth-grader should have found easy.

She blazed through the passage, seemingly effortlessly, in just 22 seconds.

But when Cohn gently questioned her, it was clear she hadn't comprehended what she'd just read.

The story of Jennie - not her real name - is one of the most common in American schools today.

She defies easy categories. She has normal intelligence. Nothing is physically wrong with her brain - no dyslexia or other "learning disabilities."

Since Jennie lives in an affluent community where the average child's IQ is 120 and most go on to college, her reading problems make her feel isolated, depressed and inadequate. Her parents don't know whether to get tough or ease off.

Kids like Jennie often become the problem students.

The Jennie in this article needs the program in Chapter One. The large number of students in Jennie's situation is creating more and more pressure on education. Students are entering society unable to understand what they read and hear around them. This reveals that education is failing to teach an important basic ability that every student needs.

Research has focussed for many years on comprehension. Great effort has been made to define what comprehension is and the specific skills necessary to develop comprehend. Because comprehension is usually measured by a student's ability to answer questions, the kinds of questions pupils must answer have been analyzed. Analysis revealed that some questions are about content, others are about interpretations of content, and others require predicting based on the content. Identification of these categories led educators to develop specific skill activities. These activities drill students on reading and answering first one and then another kind of question. Unfortunately, as noted in Chapter One, these activities test rather than teach comprehension.

Besides basic reading and spelling, numbers, and comprehension most education systems also teach writing. Educators teach students to use fundamental visual-motor skills to write numbers, letters, and do other school tasks. There are many methods for teaching basic handwriting. Most methods follow the school of thought "look at an example and copy it," over and over until it matches the example. Great creativity and effort have gone into developing fun and interesting ways for students to track their progress and for rewarding successful copies. But, the fundamental principle behind these activities is "look at it, copy it" over and over until it is correct. If a student is unable to copy successfully, after lots of practice, educators usually suggest there is a visual-motor problem. As Chapter Three discussed, educators are often limited in their ability to successfully help students with visual-motor problems. There is lots of effort to help, it is just seldom really successful.

By working to provide all students with the socially mandated basics, and then moving them through the other levels of education, educational institutions try to fulfill their mandate. Education systems and the governing agencies in societies gather numbers to prove how education is fulfilling its responsibilities.

illustration # 48
Educators and the ones who regulate education
gather numbers to try and see how education is
fulfilling its mandate.

Page for
Notes / Comments / Questions

Chapter Eight

A Real Solution

Learning and Education can add up

Most education systems come from generations of practical experience, personal investment, government investment, and research. Better international communication is also helping evolve education. Research and efforts from an education system in one nation are easily available to an education system in another nation. With these resources and background it seems reasonable to expect education is reaching the numbers its mandate requires.

To think about the results of the efforts of education, some terms need to be defined. For instance, some nations claim, through the work of their education systems, to have over ninety percent literacy in their population. Other nations don't even track the levels of literacy in their population. In any case, how many people are literate depends on how literacy is defined. At one point in history a literate person was someone able to sign their name and recite some memorized verse. This is not the modern definition of literacy.

For this book, literacy is having enough of the basic skills {reading,

illustration # 49
Basic skills help some people; the inability to use
basic skills are a burden for others.

spelling, comprehending, and writing) to get successfully through education. "Successfully," for this book, means studying any subjects of interest and having the ability to change education subjects freely because of good basic skills. Good basic skills assure the chance for success in learning other knowledge. Successful, in short, will mean persons are free to live their lives and follow their goals without interference from basic learning or literacy problems.

Numbers describing the success of education will be drawn from the United States of America. This nation, one of the largest and wealthiest in the world, has a history of compulsory education for the rising generation. Presently, the United States spends a yearly dollar amount larger than the national budget of some countries on education. The U.S. educational world receiving these dollars covers the range from local school houses to a national ministry devoted solely to education.

Section One of this book introduced Jenny, John, Mary, and some others. Each of them, as citizens of the United States, experienced different parts of the enormous U.S. education system. Their experiences mean that, at least for some individuals, education is failing in its mandate to teach the basic skills. Are the difficulties of these individuals just isolated cases? Do the difficulties of Jenny, John, Mary, and the others happen to anyone else in the U.S. education system?

It is safe to start by saying that the U.S. views itself as having learning and literacy problems. Regularly, television in the U.S. offers reports on the problems of dyslexia and learning disabilities. These reports also often describe the educational efforts to resolve these problems. There are many studies and masses of statistics that help identify and measure the literacy problem(s) in the U.S. These studies and statistics show that a large part of the U.S. population does not learn the basic skills education is mandated to teach them.

illustration # 50
Lots of numbers can hide as much as they show.

Instead of filling the next few pages with figures and numbers, here are just a few general statistics.

Since a focus of basic skills and literacy concerns how well people live their lives, the first numbers use a list called the "Adult Performance Level."

The Adult Performance Level {APL} started in 1973 with a study by Dr. Norvell Northcutt at the University of Texas. The APL was a list of areas of competence Northcutt used as a definition of adult success. They were areas of competence adults need to cope with the responsibilities of day-to-day life. In the 1970's, using the standards of the APL, the U.S. Office of Education calculated that fifty-seven million Americans didn't have the skills to do most basic tasks. The Office of Education stated twenty-three million people lacked the competencies to function successfully in society. The other thirty-four million people could function, just not very well.

The first number means, to picture it concretely, that twenty-three cities the size of San Diego, California, or Indianapolis, Indiana, or Buffalo, New York would be filled only with people unable to function successfully in them. {Each of these cities has about one million people in it.} That doesn't even count the extra thirty-four million able to function, just not very well.

In real life terms the 1970 figures meant thirty six percent of Americans could not properly fill out a W-4 tax form. Forty four percent, almost half, of Americans looking at help wanted ads could not tell if their qualifications matched the job requirements.

This situation caused great concern and led to changes in U.S. education. New programs and teaching methods came into being. More direct and binding mandates about its responsibilities went to education. Education came up with new categories for describing students. Also a push to get "back to the basics" became part of American society.

After all this effort, the U.S. Department of Education offers these statistics for the 1980's. Twenty-seven million American adults are functionally illiterate. {This is four million more than in the 1970's.} Another forty-seven million can function, just not very well. {This is thirteen million more than in the 1970's.} Also, adult illiteracy in the U.S. is estimated to be growing at 2.25 million people each year.

This illiteracy costs the United States, and its institutions, amazing sums of money. The U.S. military spends millions of dollars each year to "dummy down" repair and operation manuals. More than 225 billion dollars are lost each year because of errors, accidents, and employee turnover from illiteracy. Sixty percent, or more, of adults in prison have literacy problems. Eighty percent of juveniles brought before a court have literacy problems. More than thirty-three percent of the entire U.S. population lacks the ability to participate in everyday adult life because of reading problems.

To move these numbers closer to real life, here are examples of what they mean. The public utility in a major mid-western city, since introducing a literacy test in 1983, must immediately reject one out of every five job applicants because of illiteracy. The United Auto Workers Union-General Motors spends $200 million every year on adult "basic" education for its members. Since 1984 the United Auto Workers Union-Ford has spent $120 million on a similar program for over 100,000 displaced and active workers. A group of eight unions in New York is spending $2 million every year on adult "basic" education for their workers and families. And a study from the University of Texas found that thirty to forty percent of first year college students read below a seventh grade level.

These figures give a picture of the extent of the literacy problem in the United States. Individual stories show the impact literacy problems have in a person's life. Jenny, John, Mary, and the others are clearly not just rare individuals. Here are three more people whose lives have been profoundly influenced by literacy and learning problems.

LISA

Lisa was in the fourth grade in a Southern, suburban, school district. She had white blond hair, green eyes, and every indication that she would grow from an attractive child to a beautiful woman. Lisa was very verbal and did well socially. She did extremely well in math but, she was not going to be promoted from the fourth grade. Lisa had a reading problem.

Her school district was part of a well-to-do community. The district was one of the most progressive in the state. But, in spite of the best efforts and creative thinking of her teachers since first grade, Lisa could not read past a first grade level. This left the school district, in its thinking, with no other choice than to send Lisa to its special services building. Special placement would keep Lisa from being evaluated the same way as other students in the district. Once she was in special placement, Lisa would not fail if her reading and spelling did not improve. Special placement was necessary at this point because, in the district curriculum, fifth grade was when school changed. Before fifth grade the focus was on teaching reading and spelling. At fifth grade, it changed to a focus on using reading and writing for studies. Since Lisa couldn't read at a fifth grade level, clearly, without special placement, she would fail.

Lisa's parents went to the building where the district was arranging to place her. At the school they found all the students with difficulties from the whole district. Most children in the building did not have trouble with reading, they had other problems. A little over half the students in the school were in wheelchairs because of neurological disorders. The deaf and visually impaired students were also in this building. Lisa's parents became alarmed because, in their half day tour of the school, they did not meet a single student with Lisa's physical and verbal abilities.

Her parents took their concerns to the School Board. They said that, although they agreed with the district Lisa would not fail academically at this school, she would struggle socially. All her daily activities would be with peers who had very different abilities than Lisa. The School Board was sympathetic, but said that Lisa couldn't read past a first grade level. Since she couldn't read well enough to participate in a regular fifth grade, special placement was the only thing to do.

Ed

Ed was living in a middle sized town in the Northwest when he went on his first date by himself. He was tall with dark hair, blue eyes, and an engaging manner. He got along well with his peers, parents, and teachers. Everyone who knew Ed was also aware that he needed extra help. Ed was slow at reading and had a hard understanding or remembering new things. To help him on his first date, and be sure he found his way, Ed's father drove him to the girl's house early in the afternoon on the day of the date. Her house was two city blocks away from Ed's house, a house he had lived in all his life. At 6:00PM his family waved Ed out the door on his first date. At 7:45PM the girl called to see if Ed was all right since he had not made it to her house. At 9:30PM Ed showed up back at his house. He had been driving since six, first trying to find the girl's house and then trying to find his way home.

Herb

Herb had been a milkman for the same company, on the same route, for thirteen years. In that time the company had not had a complaint about Herb's work and his customer base had grown steadily. Herb had done so well that his company promoted him to a new, more profitable, route. Though it was larger, the new route would take him less time because he would have other milkmen under him.

The day Herb got the news about his promotion he was hospitalized in a psychiatric facility because of depression and irrational behavior. At his release, Herb's company gave him back his old route on the condition that he get therapy. After months of expensive psychotherapy the psychiatrist found out that Herb couldn't read. This problem made the prospect of changing to a new milk route seem impossible. Herb couldn't read the new street signs, follow the written directions in his route book, or write directions for the other milkmen to follow. It all seemed so hard that Herb had gone "crazy."

These people, and the others earlier in the book, show the human side of literacy problems. These people, and the numbers above, show that education needs some help to fulfill its mandate. The programs in Section One can be an important aid to education. Just as the programs change the situation for individuals, the programs can change the situation for education.

Lisa went through the program discussed in Chapter Two during the summer between her fourth and fifth grade year. When the school tested her at the start of her fifth grade year, she was reading at a fifth grade level. Lisa continued at her regular school and, at last contact, has not needed any more special help.

Ed, using the program discussed in Chapter One, learned how to picture the layout of streets and cities. He also learned to understand what he read and successfully finished college. From a young man who could not find his way around a town he had lived in all his life, Ed became a successful manager in a fabrication plant.

Herb did not believe anything could change for him. He chose not to go through a program. The last time there was any contact with Herb he was back on his old dairy route waiting for retirement.

Just as the lives of the individuals changed, or did not change, statistics for the United States and the world can change through widespread use of the programs in Section One. Education can "get the numbers." Arco, Idaho and Santa Maria, California show some possibilities the programs offer to education systems. Education can be more successful at helping students learn the basics. Recognition of the programs from Section One, and widespread use of these methods, can help eliminate most of the learning problems we know of today.

If you want to get help, or help make the programs more widely available, contact the author through the Appendix. If you read this for pleasure, share what you have learned. These programs are another step toward helping education and learning be one in the same. The methods can save people from a life like Herb's or worse. They offer a way for millions of people to succeed with learning and education and lead better lives.

Here is a last picture. It shows the three programs and how education unfolds under the influence of the basic abilities the three programs develop. If you want more information, the Appendix starts on the next page, use it and help enrich your life or the life of someone you care about.

Index

Index

Adam 65
Albert 26, 27, 28, 30, 32, 33, 39, 41
Amanda 46, 47, 48, 59
apprenticeship 92
Arco, Idaho 85, 143
arithmetic 101, 127
attention deficit 126
auditory 29, 49, 85, 95, 97, 107
Brett 47, 48, 59
comprehend 8, 16, 18, 19, 21, 23, 24, 29, 31, 32, 33,
        39, 44, 80, 81, 83, 84, 95, 96, 107, 126,
        129, 130
dyslexia 8, 18, 52, 53, 54, 100, 124, 133
Ed 139, 141
gestalt 33, 35, 36, 38
Herb 140, 141
illiterate 136, 137
inmates 81
Iowa Tests of Basic Skills 85
Jenny 21, 22, 23, 24, 30, 32, 33, 82, 133, 137
John 44, 45, 46, 48, 133, 137
Keats 28, 29, 30, 32, 33, 39, 40
learning disability 124, 127, 133
Lisa 137, 138, 139, 141
literacy 132, 133, 136, 137, 140
Mark 68, 74
Mary 66, 67, 74, 133, 137
multimedia 93
occupational therapist 64, 66, 67

phoneme segmentation 49
phonetic 48, 51, 125
phonological awareness 49
phonological processing 49
printing 62
Santa Maria, California 86, 141
sensory integration 64, 66, 67
Stanford Achievement Test 87
statistics 9, 135, 136, 143
Valarie 29, 30, 32, 33, 39, 82
verbalize/verbalization 33, 35, 40, 41
visual-motor 18, 61, 62, 63, 64, 65, 66, 67, 68, 71,
            72, 74,75, 95, 128
visual-spatial 53, 61, 62, 63, 64, 67, 71
visualize/visualization 33, 40, 107

Appendix

Thank you for looking at this book. Please share with whoever you know that needs it the hope that they can learn and lead a richer, more independent life. Even if the programs in this book are not what they need, there is a program that can help them somewhere and relentless searching will find it.

If you would like more information, or want to get help, contact:

Lindamood-Bell Learning Processes
Corporate Headquarters
416 Higuera Street
San Luis Obispo, CA 93401

800 233 1819
805 541 3836
805 541 8756 (FAX)